Pig Pirate

The Best Booty Around

Jerry Bradley

Pig Pirate
by
Jerry Bradley

Dedication

This book is for my late Son Eli Bradley.

He was killed at 11 years old while trying to board the school bus, and now it's time to lift up his name and give back to the community in his honor—statewide, with hopes of national attention.

Acknowledgments

National Award-winning chef for a BBQ recipe at GSU

A BBQ lover. Best dish I make; Duck Confit but I win awards with BBQ? Go figure? LOL. I found my new love for BBQ during a huge Cuban event I did, where I had access to a stand-up commercial smoker big enough to fit human bodies. Man, what a piece of equipment. That beast gave me new life and a whole new passion for protein flavors.

Contents

Burnt Wood 1

The Special Ingredient 3

Magically Delicious 5

Buffalo Wing Sauce Recipe 7

    Ingredients 7

Slap Ya Mama 8

    Ingredients 8

Family Business BBQ Sauce 9

Ingredients 9

House Beefy BBQ Sauce 11

    Ingredients 11

Honey BBQ Jerry Sweet 12

    Ingredients 12

Island Sweet BBQ 13

    Ingredients 13

Down South Georgia White BBQ Sauce 14

    Ingredients 14

Who's Your Daddy, Carolina Gold BBQ 15

    Ingredients 15

    Directions 15

Da Bomb Steak Sauce 17

Pepper Vinegar Sauce 18

    Ingredients 18

Jerry's Ponzu Zing Wing Sauce 19

    Ingredients 19

Jerry's Dry Rub Seasoning 20

Ingredients 20

Chef Jerry's Easy, Quick, Mix-and-Go Sauces 21

1. Yum White Sauce 21

2. Honey Garlic Wing Glaze Sauce 21

3. Frenchy Fry Sauce 22

4. The Pig's Ranch 22

Jerry's Famous Chicken Seasoning 23

Ingredients 23

Jerry's Marinara Sauce 25

Ingredients 25

Directions 26

Jerry's Ketchups! 27

Indian 27

Bloody Mary 27

Mexican 27

Secret Sauce 27

Chipotle Lime 28

Southern 28

Sweet & Sour 28

Cherry Pepper 28

Horseradish Sauce 29

Ingredients 29

Directions 29

Pork Pastor Recipes 30

Rub 30

Sauce 31

Slow Cooked BBQ Pork 2 32

    Ingredients 32

    Directions 32

Spicy Buttermilk Fried Chicken x2 34

    Ingredients 34

    Directions 34

Classic Hush Puppies 36

    Ingredients 36

    Directions 36

Baked Vidalia Onion Dip 38

    Ingredients 38

    Directions 38

Seafood Seasoning 40

    Ingredients 40

Burnt Wood

Not the Morning Type

So why is a national-award-winning, classically French-trained chef running Student Dining? The hell if I know. I guess creative juices flow through my magically delicious hands no matter the cuisine.

I got inspired by a local (hole-in-the-wall type place would be an understatement) BBQ joint that had amazing pork, Brunswick stew, and potato salad. What really won me over was the extra bottle of sauce I bought—looking at the ingredient list, it started with "Catchup." *Not* ketchup, but CATCHUP. Now *this* is my kind of place. LOL.

In all honesty, I found my new love and spirit food (BBQ and pork) after I did a massive BAD ASS Cuban event called "Havannah Nights." That event should have won a national award, but do not get me started on that!!! Learning about Cuban food was very inspiring, and I remembered how much I love that swine. Around the same time, another local joint was being built and was all the rage, so the talk of the town was BBQ this, BBQ that. BBQ is the best. And this new joint came with a lot of swag and flair. Yeah, it's not that good. I was not impressed, and I knew I was better than this.

We had a huge smoker that could hold at least two bodies in it, and we used it every day. Well, lightbulb moment happened, and the science project began. Sauces and juice flowed through my veins—straight BBQ. To do the BBQ thing, you need sauces, rubs, wood flavors, and different flavor profiles so you have something for everyone. Meat??? What about the MEATS??? OMG!!! We must have all the meats, right down to the smoked eggs. Yes, eggs. Don't knock it until you try it. Pork? Too easy. Brisket? Of course. Turkey, chickens—hell, I smoked bologna and a pineapple.

So, challenge accepted. After two test runs with directors, VPs, GMs, and managers, I learned what the local people favored. Now, I know this is a Bud Light demographic here in southeast Georgia, but it's still a good place to start and learn what works, what needed work, or didn't work at all. The Gator Bite BBQ Sandwich was born and ready to win a national award—and this cookbook was born.

Enjoy the flavors of my Burnt Wood!

The Special Ingredient

Like Po and Po's father said in *Kung Fu Panda*, there is no special ingredient. The special ingredient is love, right? No—it's skill, will, and talent. Grandma's food was made with love though. YUMMY! There is nothing better than grandma's food made with love. I was lucky—Grandma would make the sweets all day. Yes, I am a wooden spoon survivor, and NO, I do not want to talk about it! LOL!

Man, I can smell those rhubarb muffins right now. What was I talking about? Oh yeah, the love thing. Let's keep love for those we (humans) love and keep it out of my food. As a non-celebrity special consul, national-award-winning chef, *I* am the special ingredient. Not literally—please don't eat me.

I'm at that point in my career where I've realized I need to be a teacher, a mentor, and better than all those jerks who bumped me off the three TV shows I should have been on. NOT going to name any names but... you know who you are. JK—they have no idea who I am because I didn't make the last cut or the show never got picked up. But really, it's time to pass on my knowledge and craft wisdom. I enjoy teaching more than anything now. It brings me the most joy.

When people ask me for advice, I always tell them: find someone to mentor you and stick to them like glue. Don't leave them for a $0.05 hourly increase. You have to put in your time—long days. No days off for weeks. Being yelled at, told you suck, told to hurry, dealing with wrong orders, re-cooks, re-refire tickets. Hell, just say "YES CHEF" and suck it up, Buttercup. All the holidays, working late, etc… If you don't "LOVE" it? Then this isn't for you.

Now, you can hire me as a personal chef, pay a ton of money, and I'll cook and teach at the same time. No really… I am for hire!

I wonder if anyone reading this wants to hire me to teach at a university??? I've already done a lot of guest lecturing!!! The free type. I'm like a pirate—I like my booty. $$$

Magically Delicious

So you think you can cook. You're like a pirate—you plunder others' recipes and steal them to make them your own. NO ONE, and I mean NO ONE, can BBQ as good as you. NO ONE can fry a Thanksgiving turkey like you! NO ONE can fry shrimp like you!!

I hate to tell you this, but you're full of shit.

It's not just that I'm better than you (at cooking—I'm sure you're a wonderful, kind person), but I have been gifted. After 12 years with my mentor, I became a national award-winning chef. But that came from taking the beatings until my morale improved. Taking the Tom and Jerry jokes for 12 freaking years (yes, my mentor's name was Tom—yes, I get it, Tom and Jerry, so cute, blah). After taking the abuse, being told I wasn't as good as him—I finally made it. Now I was the Executive Chef. Now I was winning awards. I am now better than everyone and no one is as good as me.

I have the Magically Delicious fingers.

You see, when my mentor made me the executive chef of one of his restaurants, he stepped aside and moved out to the front of the house.

HE STILL WON'T STOP MESSING WITH MY FOOD AND TOUCHING EVERYTHING I MADE. DAMN YOU, TOM!!! I love you though, and you know that.

See, Tom had the Magically Delicious hands—and fingers. I would make the best food—good-looking and just amazing—and he would still have to touch it, fluff it up, move one leaf here or there. JERK!! I love you, Tom!

So, Tom had the Magically Delicious hands. Just his touch would make things better.

Out on my own, I found myself doing the same thing. I ran the show. It was my menus and food. Once a cook made something, I *had* to touch it and make it Magically Delicious.

I have the magic hands now.

So a classically French-trained chef from Johnson and Wales University can play in anyone's yard now that I've got these magic hands. I won a national award with BBQ? Get out of town!

So these magic hands wish to share these recipes with you. Don't try to cook around me—I'll take over or use it as a teaching moment! LOL!!

I wish you well and good luck. Google me if you need inspiration.

Buffalo Wing Sauce Recipe

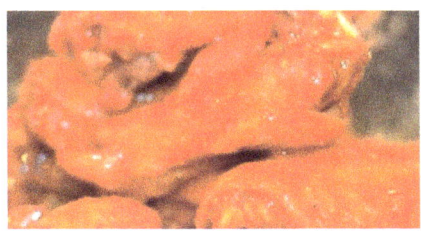

Ingredients

- 4 lbs butter
- 6 cups hot sauce (Texas Pete)
- 5 teaspoons ground red pepper
- 3 teaspoons cayenne pepper
- 2 tablespoons Tabasco

Melt the butter in a saucepan. Add the hot sauce, cayenne pepper, ground red pepper, and Tabasco. Whisk to combine.

Slap Ya Mama

Ingredients

- 2 cups apple cider vinegar
- 1 cup ketchup
- 4 tablespoons brown sugar
- 2 tablespoons Worcestershire sauce
- 4 tablespoons barbecue rub
- 2 teaspoons paprika
- 4 teaspoons salt
- ½ teaspoon black pepper

Combine all ingredients. Best if stored in a cool place for 24 hours, but can be used immediately.

Family Business BBQ Sauce

Ingredients

- 3 cups catchup
- 3 cups white vinegar
- ⅓ cup dry mustard
- ⅓ cup sugar
- ¼ pound butter
- ¼ cup Tabasco
- 3 tablespoons black pepper
- 3 tablespoons sea salt
- ½ cup Worcestershire sauce

Mix all ingredients *except* the vinegar and mustard. Bring to a slow boil. Whisk the vinegar and mustard together in a bowl to form a paste, then add to the mixture and simmer for 30 minutes.

Don't mistake my kindness for weakness. I am kind to everyone, but when someone is unkind to me, weak is not what you are going to remember about me.

– Al Capone

nothing personal

just business

House Beefy BBQ Sauce

Ingredients

- 4 cups ketchup
- 2 cups apple cider vinegar
- 1 cup brown sugar
- 4 tablespoons Worcestershire sauce
- 2 teaspoons garlic salt

Combine all ingredients and enjoy!

Honey BBQ Jerry Sweet

Ingredients

- 1 cup ketchup
- ⅓ cup white vinegar
- ¼ cup molasses
- ¼ cup local wildflower honey (slightly warmed)
- 1 teaspoon liquid smoke
- ½ teaspoon salt
- ½ teaspoon black pepper
- ¼ teaspoon paprika
- ¼ teaspoon chili powder
- ¼ teaspoon onion powder
- ¼ teaspoon garlic powder

Thoroughly mix all ingredients (slightly warm the honey first). Let sit at room temperature for 24 hours. Mix again—and it's ready to go!

Island Sweet BBQ

Ingredients

- 5 cups ketchup
- 1 cup tomato paste
- 6 cups white vinegar
- 6 cups pineapple juice
- 5 cups sugar
- 1½ cups soy sauce
- 6 teaspoons powdered ginger
- 1½ cups Texas Pete sauce
- ½ cup Sriracha
- 5–10 drops red food coloring

Mix all ingredients together and serve. This sauce is very sweet, so use with care on the BBQ—better for basting and tossing than long grilling.

Down South Georgia White BBQ Sauce

Ingredients

- 1½ cups Duke's mayo
- ½ cup apple cider vinegar
- 2 tablespoons lemon juice
- 3 teaspoons Dijon mustard
- 3 teaspoons Frank's Hot Sauce
- 1½ teaspoons Worcestershire sauce
- 2 teaspoons honey
- 1 teaspoon garlic powder
- 1 teaspoon onion powder
- 2 teaspoons salt
- ¼ teaspoon white pepper
- ½ teaspoon black pepper

Mix all ingredients together. Let chill for 1 hour. Even better after 24 hours.

Who's Your Daddy, Carolina Gold BBQ

Ingredients

- 1 cup French's yellow mustard
- ½ cup sugar
- ¼ cup brown sugar
- 1 cup apple cider vinegar
- 2 tablespoons chili powder
- 2 teaspoons Sriracha sauce
- 2 teaspoons black pepper
- ½ teaspoon soy sauce
- ½ teaspoon cayenne pepper
- 2 tablespoons melted butter
- 1 teaspoon liquid smoke

Directions

- Mix all ingredients together—easy peasy!
- If it's too thick, add a little water.
- If you like it tangier, add more mustard or vinegar—your choice!

FOR SALE: WORLD'S GREATEST BRUNSWICK STEW RECIPE
THE FIRST-EVER RECIPE FROM BRUNSWICK, GA
WITH THE JERRY FLAIR

Da Bomb Steak Sauce

This one's for the people. Jerry and the Pirate Pig don't care for steak sauces, but I'm here to please the masses.

Ingredients

- 1½ cups water
- 1 cup balsamic vinegar
- 1 cup Worcestershire sauce
- 1½ cups ketchup
- 1 teaspoon celery seed
- 2 teaspoons kosher salt
- 1 teaspoon black pepper
- 2 tablespoons chili sauce
- 1 tablespoon minced garlic
- ½ large yellow onion, minced

Bring all ingredients to a slow simmer and let it cook for about 10 minutes—look for a slow rolling boil. Once done, refrigerate for at least 12 hours.

Note: Don't ask me how it should taste—I don't care for it, *LOL!* But hey, they tell me it's nice!

Pepper Vinegar Sauce

Ingredients

- ½ cup tomato paste
- 1 tablespoon minced garlic
- 4 oz tomato sauce
- ½ cup apple cider vinegar
- 2 tablespoons black pepper
- 1 tablespoon honey
- 1 tablespoon chili powder
- 1 teaspoon cayenne pepper
- ½ teaspoon cumin
- 2 tablespoons melted butter
- 1 tablespoon Worcestershire sauce

Melt the butter in a microwave-safe dish. Mix all ingredients except the vinegar. Once it forms a pasty mixture, add the vinegar last. Adjust by adding more vinegar to taste.

Jerry's Ponzu Zing Wing Sauce

Ingredients

- 2 cups hoisin sauce
- 2 cups soy sauce
- 1 cup key lime juice
- 2 tablespoons sesame oil
- 2 tablespoons green curry paste
- ½ cup sugar
- ½ cup honey
- 2 tablespoons Sriracha sauce
- ½ cup fresh orange juice
- Sliced scallions, mixed sesame seeds, and cilantro for garnish (optional)

Combine all ingredients until smooth. Adjust key lime juice for a tangier flavor. Adjust Sriracha sauce for more heat. Adjust sugar and honey for added sweetness.

Jerry's Dry Rub Seasoning

Ingredients

- 2 cups sea salt
- ½ cup cayenne pepper
- ½ cup dry mustard
- ½ cup black pepper
- 1 cup garlic powder
- 1 cup onion powder
- 1 cup ground red pepper
- ½ cup celery salt
- 2 cups Caribbean jerk seasoning

Chef Jerry's Easy, Quick, Mix-and-Go Sauces

1. Yum White Sauce

Ingredients

- 2 cups real whipped mayo
- ½ cup ketchup
- 3 tablespoons granulated sugar
- 1 tablespoon garlic powder
- 1 tablespoon paprika
- 1 teaspoon salt
- 1 teaspoon onion powder
- 1 teaspoon white vinegar

2. Honey Garlic Wing Glaze Sauce

Ingredients

- 1 cup melted margarine
- 1 tablespoon minced garlic
- ¼ cup honey
- ½ cup Frank's Hot Sauce
- ¼ cup ketchup

3. Frenchy Fry Sauce

Ingredients

- ¾ cup real mayo
- 1 cup ketchup
- ½ cup Statesboro Buffalo Wing Sauce
- 1 tablespoon pickle brine (juice)
- 1 teaspoon paprika
- ½ teaspoon salt

4. The Pig's Ranch

Ingredients

- ½ cup real mayo
- ½ cup sour cream
- ½ cup buttermilk
- ¼ cup pickle brine
- ½ teaspoon dill
- ½ teaspoon parsley
- ½ teaspoon fresh chives
- ½ teaspoon onion powder
- ½ teaspoon garlic powder
- ½ teaspoon fine sea salt
- ¼ teaspoon black pepper
- 3 teaspoons fresh lemon juice

Jerry's Famous Chicken Seasoning

Ingredients

- 1 cup lemon pepper
- 1 cup black pepper
- 1 cup white pepper
- 1 quart granulated garlic
- 1 quart onion powder
- 1 cup sage
- ¼ cup paprika
- 1 cup cayenne pepper
- 1 box salt

Mix All Ingredients in a Bowl and Serve

Jerry's Marinara Sauce

Ingredients

- 2 cups olive oil
- 2 bags of small diced onions (#5)
- 1 quart minced garlic (32 oz)
- 2 cans (#10) stewed tomatoes
- 2 cans (#10) fire-roasted diced tomatoes
- 1¼ cup oregano
- 1½ cups salt
- 1¼ cups pepper
- 1 can (#10) tomato paste

Directions

- Sweat the onions with the olive oil in a steam kettle on high heat.
- Add all ingredients except the tomato paste.
- Cook down on medium heat for 15–20 minutes.
- Add the tomato paste and stir well.
- Turn off heat and let sit for 10 minutes.
- Burr mix until smooth (no chunks).

Jerry's Ketchups!

Indian

- ½ cup ketchup
- ¼ cup sautéed tomatoes
- ½ tsp curry powder

Bloody Mary

- ½ cup ketchup
- 1 tsp Tabasco
- 1 tsp horseradish
- ½ tsp celery salt

Mexican

- ½ cup ketchup
- 2 tbsp Cholula sauce

Secret Sauce

- ½ cup ketchup
- ½ tbsp brown mustard
- ½ cup mayo
- 3 cornichons, chopped

Chipotle Lime

- ½ cup ketchup
- 1 canned chipotle in adobo, chopped
- ½ tbsp fresh lime juice

Southern

- ½ cup ketchup
- ½ cup sautéed onion
- 2 tbsp brown sugar
- 1 tsp liquid smoke

Sweet & Sour

- ½ cup ketchup
- ¼ cup apple cider vinegar
- ¼ cup brown sugar

Cherry Pepper

- ½ cup ketchup
- ½ cup pitted halved cherries
- ¼ tsp cracked black pepper

Horseradish Sauce

Ingredients

- 1 cup sour cream
- ½ cup grated fresh horseradish
- 1 tbsp Dijon-style mustard
- 1 tsp white wine vinegar
- ½ tsp garlic salt

Directions

- To make the sauce, place all of the ingredients into a medium mixing bowl and whisk together until the mixture is smooth and creamy.
- Cover the bowl with a lid or aluminum foil and chill for at least 4 hours or overnight.
- This allows the flavors to meld.
- This sauce can be stored in the refrigerator for up to 3 weeks, tightly covered.
- Makes about 1¼ cups of sauce.

Pork Pastor Recipes

Rub

- ⅔ cup oregano
- ⅔ cup cumin
- 2 cups chipotle powder
- 1 cup garlic powder
- ½ cup salt
- ½ cup pepper
- ½ cup cocoa powder
- 4 cups granulated sugar

Sauce

- 1 gallon chicken stock
- ⅓ cup red wine vinegar
- 2 cups minced garlic
- ¼ Salt
- 1⅓ cups sugar
- 2 gallons bacon with grease
- 6 (7 oz) cans chipotle peppers
- 1 (16 oz) can green chilies

Blend with immersion blender until smooth.

Slow Cooked BBQ Pork 2

Ingredients

- 1 (2 lb) boneless pork butt roast
- 2 cups apple juice
- 1 (18 oz) bottle BBQ sauce
- 1 large Vidalia (sweet) onion, sliced
- 4 cloves garlic, minced
- $\frac{1}{4}$ cup melted butter
- 8 hamburger buns
- Pickles

Directions

- Preheat a slow cooker or large Dutch oven on low.
- Add the pork roast and pour the apple juice over the top.
- Sprinkle the onion and garlic over the top and around sides, cover with the lid and let cook on low for 6 to 8 hours.

- Meat is done when it shreds easily when pulled apart between 2 forks. Pour the bottle of sauce over the shredded meat and mix well.

- Using a brush, cover insides of buns with melted butter and toast lightly in oven.

- Serve the meat on toasted buns with homemade coleslaw if desired.

- Makes 8 sandwiches.

Spicy Buttermilk Fried Chicken

Ingredients

- 2 cups all-purpose flour
- ½ tsp salt
- ¼ tsp freshly ground black pepper
- 1½ to 2 tsp cayenne pepper
- 1 tsp garlic powder
- ½ tsp paprika
- 1 cup buttermilk
- 2½ to 3 lbs chicken pieces

Directions

- In a large bowl, combine the flour, salt, black pepper, cayenne pepper, garlic powder, and paprika.
- Place the buttermilk in a shallow pie plate.
- Dredge the chicken in the flour mixture, then dip in the buttermilk, then back in the flour mixture.
- In a deep, heavy Dutch oven, heat 1½ inches of vegetable oil to 350°F.

- Using tongs, carefully add a few pieces of chicken to the Dutch oven.

- Fry for 12 to 15 minutes, or until the chicken is no longer pink and the coating is golden brown, turning once.

- Drain on paper towels and keep warm in a 300°F oven while frying the remaining pieces.

- Makes 6 servings.

Classic Hush Puppies

Ingredients

- 1 cup yellow cornmeal
- ¾ cup self-rising flour
- ¾ tsp garlic salt
- ½ tsp baking soda
- ½ cup finely chopped Vidalia onion
- 1 tbsp chopped green onion
- ¾ cup buttermilk
- 1 large egg
- Vegetable oil for frying

Directions

- In a medium bowl, combine cornmeal, flour, garlic salt, and baking soda. Add both onions and stir well.
- In a small bowl, whisk together the buttermilk and egg until smooth. Add to the cornmeal mixture, whisking to combine.
- In a Dutch oven, pour oil to a depth of 2 inches.

- Heat to 325°F. Drop batter by tablespoons into the hot oil.

- Fry for 3–4 minutes or until golden brown on all sides. Remove with a slotted spoon and drain on paper towels. Serve warm.

Baked Sweet 6A Onion Dip

Ingredients

- 1 large Vidalia onion, chopped
- 1 cup grated Swiss cheese
- 1 cup mayonnaise
- 1 clove garlic, minced
- 1 tsp hot pepper sauce
- ½ cup grated Parmesan cheese

Directions

- These large, mild, and sweet onions are prevalent in South Georgia, but any sweet, mild onion will do.
- Preheat the oven to 375°F.
- Combine the first five ingredients in a medium bowl and spread into a shallow baking dish.
- Sprinkle the top evenly with the Parmesan cheese.
- Bake for 25 minutes, or until the edges are bubbly and the top is golden brown.

- Serve warm with a variety of crackers or consider adding crudités like carrots, radishes, celery, etc.
- Makes 2 cups.

Seafood Seasoning

The traditional seafood seasoning used today originated in the Baltimore area and was first used for steaming large pots of hard-shelled crabs. Today, it's a Southern staple, used in salads, Low Country boils, sprinkled over freshly steamed shrimp, broiled fish, and even French fries. It can be bought premade, but if your area doesn't carry a product like this, here's an excellent homemade recipe.

Ingredients

- 1 cup celery salt
- 4 tbsp sweet paprika
- 4 bay leaves, finely ground
- 2 tsp black pepper
- 2 tsp cayenne (red) pepper
- 1 tsp dry mustard
- 1 tsp mace
- ½ tsp cinnamon
- ½ tsp allspice
- 8 whole cloves, finely ground
- ½ tsp ground ginger

Directions

- Grind the bay leaves and cloves using a coffee or spice grinder.

- Place all ingredients in a tightly sealed zip-top bag and shake well to mix evenly.

- Store the seasoning in a tightly sealed jar in a cool, dry, and dark place. It will keep for several months.

About the Author

National award-winning special chef consul and Executive Chef, Jerry Bradley is classically French-trained—yet still makes a mean frozen pizza. He has studied coast to coast, border to border, trends, and cuisines, and has cooked for a president, movie stars, rock stars, famous athletes, WWE superstars, political figures, and the ultra-wealthy.

Despite his accolades, he remains grounded—currently running campus dining, where he opened the country's largest dining hall and created a wonderland of food for freshman college kids.